NATIONAL GEOGRAPHIC

T0069720

Food Comes From Farms

Miles Taylor

Do you know where the food you eat comes from? Most of the food comes from farms.

peanut butter
bread
apple

The bread is made from wheat.

Farmers grow wheat on farms.

The peanut butter **is made from peanuts.**

Farmers grow peanuts on farms.

The milk comes from cows.

Farmers keep cows on farms.

The apple comes from an apple tree.

Farmers grow apple trees on farms.

People need farms. Most of the food we eat comes from farms.